Cousins Camp

A Guide To Spending Special Time

With Your Grandchildren

Updated 2019

By

Jana Dube Hletko

ISBN-10: 154303652X

ISBN-13: 978-1543036527

Cover design, interior layout, and editing by Lynn Zacny Busby

Back cover photo and professional photos on page 13 and 95 by Mary Guajardo, Mary G. Images

Front cover photo by Sarah Hletko Donahue

Other photography by Jana Hletko

Cartoon on page 11 reprinted with permission:
Family Circus: © 2007 Bill Keane, Inc. Distributed by King Features Syndicate

Notice: Every effort has been made to locate the copyright owners of material used in this book. Please let us know of any error, and we will gladly make any necessary corrections in subsequent printings.

Printed in the United States of America

This book is available through Amazon.com and other fine booksellers.

Dedication

This book is dedicated to my three children, their spouses, their children (our nine wonderful grandchildren), and my husband, without whom NONE of this would have been possible.

In addition, I want to give a special shout-out to my college roommate and best friend in the whole world, Lynn Zacny Busby. This book would not have happened without her pushing, prodding, AND computer skills.

COUSINS CAMP

Version 2.0

A Guide To Spending Special Time
With Your Grandchildren

Introduction

When I decided to host a Cousins Camp for my grandchildren, I started to plan and visualize what it might look like. I knew I wanted some special time with my grandchildren, but my vision was a little blurry. This book is the culmination of things I have done in our nine years of Cousins Camp. I hope you will be able to benefit from some of my trials and errors and perhaps use some of these ideas.

When I was a high school English teacher, I spent a lot of time planning my lessons. Though I looked at countless available lesson plans in many sources, I found the most effective strategy was to get a few ideas and then "invent my own wheel." I found I just couldn't do things the way someone else did; I had to make it my own. As a matter of fact, even when I taught the same thing I had taught before (such as *Romeo and Juliet*), I rarely used the exact lesson plan twice. I altered and adjusted, added and subtracted to make each year fit the class.

I hope that is what you will do with this book. The Cousins Camp that I run for my grandchildren will probably not look like your camp at all. There are too many variations: where your grandchildren live, where you live, transportation concerns, numbers of grandchildren, your budget, even what you call your camp.

However, you will be able to save planning time and hopefully improve your time with your grandchildren by looking at what I have done and then molding it to work for your situation.

As a matter of fact, you may not even run a camp for cousins. You may have just one or two grandchildren who are in the same family. You may decide to just have your grandchildren come to your house for a few hours.... Or a few hours a day, several days in a row. Or.... You see the point: Your special time with your grandchildren will take on qualities of its own.

Note: The Important Thing Is To Spend Some Special Time Together.

When I first heard one of my neighbors refer to her camp, I immediately knew I wanted to do the same thing. Her name is Kirby, and she calls her camp Camp Kirby. Since then, I have heard of Grandma Camp, Cousin Camp, and various other names for the get-togethers that grandmothers host. My first few ideas came from Kirby, and I will forever thank her. If not for that quick conversation, my grandchildren and I might not have ever made the incredible memories that have come from our Cousins Camp.

You have clearly already thought about doing something special with your grandchildren; I hope this book will help you decide how some of that time will look.

I have learned that some grandparents have specific agendas for their camps. Some are concerned about manners or religion or teaching healthy eating. My sole concern is that we have a good time in a healthy, safe environment.

I want them to know how much my husband and I love them; we enjoy talking about last year's Cousins Camp and next year's Cousins Camp when we see them at other times of the year. I hope they will always remember Cousins Camp and the time we have spent together.

While I do not fill the cousins with junk food or allow them to stay up all night, I do have some leeway. After all, making them healthy, productive adults is a job best done by their parents.

So, in general, I serve healthy meals with lots of fruits and vegetables, though we do eat the occasional lunch at a fast food restaurant. And yes, once I did let them have corn dogs for breakfast! But, really, that was just once. See the MEALS section for some recipes that have worked. The more things you can do ahead or do simply, the happier you will be.

"Can you pretend you're Grandma just once and give us whatever we want?"

Because my nine grandchildren all live far away, I have always looked for ways that my husband and I could be part of their lives. I wanted to create memories that would last for their whole lives. I wanted to make sure the cousins would know us AND would know each other.

Of our three adult children, two families live in the Chicago area and one family lives in Washington, DC. With demanding careers, active schedules, and financial considerations, it is not always easy for them to get together. Cousins Camp provides one answer. Because of the distances involved (my husband and I live in South Carolina), that means my camp has to be a sleep-over, multi-day affair.

Kirby's children bring the grandchildren to her as they are all within driving distance. The parents also come back to pick them up. She usually has at least one parent stay to help her through the week.

My friend Debbie has grandchildren in the Midwest AND the Northeast. She collects the Midwest child and drives to pick up the two in the Northeast. They then take a ferry to Nantucket where the fun begins. That sounds really difficult to me, but she says the kids are great and so excited about the special time with Grandma and Grandpa. Gosh, I would be, too.

I'm afraid her trip will get more complicated as the youngest two Midwesterners are old enough to join the fun. Two cars? Planes? I will wait to hear how she solves the problem. What I am sure of though is that she will continue to spend special time with her grandchildren on Nantucket, a place she and her husband love. I'll bet all her grandchildren will love it, too.

Andrew coloring his new flip-flops

Important Paperwork

My children expect that we will take very good care of their children. While we have been very fortunate that no one has gotten sick or hurt during Cousins Camp (just a second, I have to knock on wood), we plan ahead and have the parents sign Permission to Seek Medical Treatment forms. These include all appropriate names and medical insurance policies.

Our notes have not been official. Since almost everyone has cell phones now, it should be easy to get hold of a parent if necessary. However, it is a good idea to have signed permissions for travel and/or medical treatment--- just in case. If you are taking children out of the country or the parents will not be easily available, you may want to check with a lawyer for the proper forms. They may need to be notarized or follow a particular format. I think it is a good idea to be completely prepared on this issue.

Be sure to get a list of medications that a child may need. Have the parent include the name of the medication, the dose and the way it must be administered. For example: Should the medicine be given at a particular time and should it be given with or without food? Medications should be in original bottles with childproof caps.

Note: Do not pack any medicines in checked baggage.

Homesickness

Be aware that homesickness could be a problem. That is one of the reasons we didn't have children attend Cousins Camp until they had finished kindergarten. We tried to avert the homesickness issue by allowing phone calls anytime and always at night. If the request for a phone call came too early in the day, I would distract them with a hug and a kiss and tell them "We'll call in a few minutes." Parents could, of course, call us here, too. The kids like it when I take a picture of them doing something special and send it right off to a parent's phone. At night, you might lie down for a few minutes with a child who is a little upset. You could also make a little calendar to show them when they will be going home and mark off the days. With Skype and FaceTime, parents really aren't far away.

So, How Should You Start?

My job here is to get you started thinking about what your camp will look like. I hope to provide ideas for you to incorporate into your activities. I know you will come up with many ideas of your own as well.

Because I made this decision while my grandchildren were still young -- and, of course, there were not 9 of them at the beginning --I took Kirby's suggestion and said that cousins would be eligible for Camp upon completion of kindergarten. At the time, I also said once a grandchild turned 10, they would no longer be eligible. Kirby's grandchildren were already approaching their teen years, and she found the boys' roughhousing and the teen issues a little too much to deal with. There is also the consideration of mixing the big kids with little kids. She has tried having one camp for girls and one for boys. You could also do one camp for younger kids and one for older ones. That would have defeated my purpose of having the cousins all know each other, so I decided against those options.

Of course, rules are to be broken, right? We will get back to that! Our original rules meant that our first Cousins Camp had two campers-- our son's oldest child, Sofie, and our youngest daughter's oldest child, Andrew. I was immediately confronted with the transportation issue. Since those two families live in the Chicago area, I had to get the children to South Carolina.

My solution was to fly to Chicago, collect the two children the next day, and fly back home. Five days later, my husband and I flew to Chicago, gave the children to their parents (whew!) and spent a few days of rest before returning home.

Hint: I purchased my first round trip ticket (MYR-ORD) for the first day I flew to Chicago to pick them up and my return ticket for the day my husband and I flew home at the end of the whole trip. My second round trip ticket (ORD-MYR) was for the identical days I was flying with the children. That way my ticket matched theirs and there would be less chance for confusion as we went through security.

As I already mentioned, the parents signed a note that we had permission to take their children out of state. We did not make them get the notes notarized, but that may have been a good idea.

That worked well for the first two years. For year three, we added two more campers. Then for the fourth year of camp, one more camper joined us. YES, I flew from Chicago to Myrtle Beach with five children!

That solved our transportation for the first years though it became very expensive as more round trip tickets were added each year. Luckily, we have low cost Spirit Airlines, which flies non-stop between Myrtle Beach and Chicago.

NOTE: *After the third and fourth child joined us, we had to rent a minivan as I had only five available seat belts. Due to their ages and heights, our children could not ride in the front seat, and I had camp counselors to help me, so we certainly did not fit in our car. You will need appropriate car seats/booster seats/seat belts for your whole group.*

For the first five years, we had matching t-shirts. I purchased mine from Custom Ink (see Resources). Their associates are extremely helpful. I chose the design the first year and stuck with it through the years, just changing the number of stick figures, the dates, and the shirt colors. I wish I had included little stick figures for our dogs, but it never occurred to me until now.

When I did change the shirt the year we met in Chicago, I added a city skyline. The date, Cousins Camp name, and figures of children (instead of the stick figures) were still there, but the children ALL complained that they liked our "REAL" t-shirts more.

Besides being a great reminder to the children of the fun we have, this is a wonderful way to spot your group in a crowd. We wear them anytime we go out. I use a marker to put their names on the tag so we don't get them mixed up in the wash. We have had red, green, yellow, blue, and purple shirts.

After this picture was taken, the TSA agent must have felt really sorry for me because he let us go through the employee line so we didn't have to wait. Another time, we got free ice cream cones at a fast food restaurant. The kids were thrilled.

In 2013, we decided to host camp in Chicago where we have a small apartment, which limited the airline tickets and the need to rent a van. Even if we had to rent some sort of extended stay suite hotel, it would have been cheaper than all the airline tickets and rental car. In Chicago, we have great public transportation available, and the children even ride free.

That year should have marked the end of camp, according to the original rules, for the two oldest grandchildren. Therefore, we should have had three campers in attendance. But, the older two were quite upset, so we decided we could include them for one more year (watch what happens the next year!). Remember: Rules are to be broken sometimes.

We then decided to invite the sixth Chicago grandchild even though she hadn't finished kindergarten since camp would last only 3 nights. Because there was no transportation time necessary, and our apartment is small, that seemed like the appropriate amount of time. Of course, we invited the oldest grandchild from DC to join us even though she was just about to start kindergarten. Unfortunately, the timing didn't work for her, so there were six grandchildren for camp.

City camp presented its own challenges. First of all, I could not hire my regular camp counselors. My husband became my partner in activities, meal presentations, and everything in between. He was fabulous! Though he wasn't much help with the crafts or bedtime, he was the main person in charge of meals and clean up. And he loved Bingo!

There was one little incident: He got distracted at the Museum of Science and Industry, which was our major outing. We had to take a bus, and I had asked my sister-in-law to go with us so we would have one adult in charge of two children. After just 15 minutes at the museum, I saw our oldest two grandchildren, but NOT my husband.

Once we found him (he explained he was reading a VERY interesting discussion of a display), I put the two children in charge of him. The rest of the day was fine. We enjoyed many displays, including chickens hatching, a great tornado/wind activity, and some rock climbing. If I were to do it again, I would access the museum map and plan out our visit strategy instead of wandering.

We had hoped for good weather as we waited for the bus to go to the Museum of Science and Industry. We got lucky on the way there, but it did begin to rain while we waited.... And waited... for the bus to return home. My sister-in-law said she took a two-hour nap when she got home.

I knew that we would have to keep them very busy in our apartment and found several Minute To Win It games that could be inserted into our schedule anytime necessary. We made Lava Lamps, Dream Catchers, and wonderful notes for their parents (Why My Dad is the Best Dad and a newspaper page of Things I Love About my Mother).[1] We played Bingo, went to the movies and went bowling.

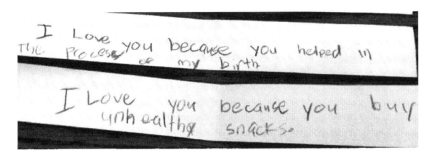

(I love you because you helped in the process of my birth)
(I love you because you buy unhealthy snacks.)

Our son cut out his comments from his Why My Dad is the Best Dad gift and posted them on Facebook.

---

[1] http://www.marthastewart.com/341027/mothers-day-newspaper

This was certainly different from going to the beach and pool, but it was equally wonderful. The kids said they were worried about how camp would work in Chicago, but they were glad to find out that we had crafts and games planned. Though we missed playing outside as much as we had other years, we had a great time. Of course, even if you live in a city, you probably have parks nearby. And a trip to a zoo is a great outing. I had planned for us to go to the Lincoln Park Zoo, but we didn't do that because a couple of the kids had just gone to the zoo with some friends.

PQ and Sofie playing Bingo

At the end of camp in 2013, I was a little bit stymied. Our Washington, DC grandchildren would be old enough to attend camp in 2014, but I just couldn't think of a way to overcome the transportation issues.

After all, I couldn't possibly collect children in two cities. In addition, I just didn't think my husband and I could adequately care for so many children for several days. How would we get to the beach, the pool, ANYWHERE with so many children? How would we ever get them to bed?

After hours of agonizing over this problem, I finally came up with the solution.

Cousins Camp Morphs To Family Camp

Instead of Cousins Camp, camp in 2014 would be a Family Camp. Of course, the emphasis would still be on the cousins, but parents would attend also. That way, families would arrive and leave together; parents would be responsible for the day-to-day stuff like laundry, baths, bed time. There would be plenty of cars, seatbelts, and age-appropriate car seats.

So, we set the date and kept our fingers crossed that everyone could arrange their schedules.... And that no hurricane would interrupt our fun.... And began to plan for Cousins Camp during the first week of August. It is important to set the date early for the best chance of getting everyone together.

I am happy to report that Cousins Camp 2014 was a huge success. It took a lot of advance planning to have 17 people at our house for a week. Yes, it was a whole week! But, the reality was that my husband and I were not nearly as exhausted at the end of the week as in past years.

Sleeping arrangements included lots of blow-up beds. I have three and was able to borrow more from my friend Kirby (Thank you again, Kirby). It took days before camp to figure out and wash bedding and towels. I did have to buy a few towels but they continue to be used each year. Each family was responsible for their own clean clothes and towels. The washing machine and dryer were in CONSTANT use.

We made no attempt to go anywhere in a group. I can't imagine trying to move 17 people in a group. We just announced that families could be responsible for their own children if they wanted to go somewhere. I made a list of possible outings so they would know what is available.

Some went to the discount malls and some went to Wonder Works (an interactive museum in Myrtle Beach), but in general the fun was at the beach, the pool, and playing with the cousins. Our 18-month old granddaughter was a huge hit with all the older cousins and kept everyone very entertained. She continues to be a center of attraction and will be 6 years old for Cousins Camp 2019.

We made no attempt to go out to eat. Again, moving 17 people is just not an easy feat. Besides being expensive, it isn't much fun to take that big a group out to dinner. No one gets to sit and talk because there is always someone chasing a child. At our house, though, mealtime was a great time for the adults to visit while the children ate at their own table and laughed and joked with each other.

I cooked and froze several meals ahead of time. I made some dinner casseroles and also some breakfast casseroles. I made lists on a yellow pad of menus and what I would have to do each day. Last year, I typed up my list and posted it on the refrigerator for easy reference. (See pages 94-96.) The more you can do ahead, the more you will enjoy your family time.

Though I knew we would have to order in several times, I wanted to avoid the yawn factor of ordering pizza. I came up with theme nights. We had a Hawaiian luau, an Italian night, and a Mexican night.

For the luau, we had leis, fancy paper tablecloths, flower barrettes for the girls, and straws with "flowers" on them.

Eloise wearing her Luau flower barrette the next morning.

I served barbecue ribs (from our local take-out restaurant), barbecued chicken sandwiches (see crock pot recipe under Food section), several salads from our local grocery store, ambrosia salad that I made and coconut cake that I purchased from a local baker. The kids' drinks were 7-up that I tinted blue with a Swedish fish swimming in the clear plastic cup. They were very excited to be drinking "ocean water."

For Italian night, we ordered pizza and subs from another local take-out. I added salads and fruits; for dessert we had miniature cannoli from our local grocery store. We had chef's hats and mustaches. We used red checked paper tablecloths and red plastic plates. We had Italian flags and a photo op.

Lucille (left) and Sabine (right) standing on a small stool behind the Ole Pizza Shoppe banner taped to the entrance doorway of our kitchen.

For Mexican night, we had great paper tablecloths and napkins, flags strung across the kitchen, little rubber duckies with sombreros for the kids to keep. The food that night came from our local Mexican take-out restaurant.

One night, we had a lovely catered dinner (don't picture fancy, just really good!). As we sat down to dinner, one of the grandchildren looked around and said, "But, Grandma, what is our theme tonight?"

Each night, the children helped with the decorations and setting the table. They all wanted to help and had a great time showing things off to their parents, who feigned total surprise.

I love to think about possible themes. We have had a Western night, a Chinese night, a French night, a Mardi Gras night, and a birthday celebration. For that night we sat by people who have the same birthday months instead of an adult table and a kids table. That mixed things up a little and took care of my wish to celebrate at least one birthday together during the year!

Now that you are thinking and planning, let's get on to some of the specifics.

"Sleep Dust"

When the grandchildren were very young, I started providing Sleep Dust at bedtime. Sleep dust is administered after the children have brushed teeth, had their nighttime story and been tucked into bed (Brush,

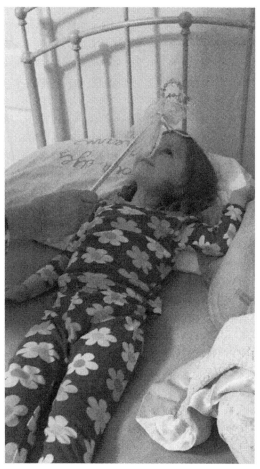

Book, Bed). I arrive with a small fairy wand in hand and say something like: "Night, night, little girl (boy). I'm so glad you have come to South Carolina, and I hope you are having a very good time." I trail the little ribbons down their face. My wand has a small heart that dangles, and I let them hold the heart and make a wish. Then, I give them a small gift, kiss them, and say "Good Night."

I always thought it helped everyone settle down and want to go to bed quickly. It was invaluable when I was the person in charge and very tired at the end of the day! Sleep dust gifts are things like a key chain, a bottle of bubbles for the next day, a book, a bath toy, a shark tooth necklace, a craft for the next day, a card game, a puzzle. Sometimes, I might get a more expensive gift as a family group gift..... e.g. a book of poems, a book of science experiments, an ant farm. Last year, I froze one dollar coins in ice cube trays. The kids all thought the cold, hard cash was great and could hardly wait for the ice to melt.

Obviously, the list is varied and endless. I avoid giving candy.

Hint: Put sleep dust presents in separate bags and label them for which night. For example, if you want to paint rocks on Tuesday, the rock sets could be sleep dust on Monday night.

Camp Counselor(s)

I recommend hiring high school students to help with the children. When we had just two campers, I hired a young girl who lives across the street to help when we went on a field trip or to the pool or beach. She worked just a few hours when I needed her.

Once we had more campers, I had to get more organized with the counselor situation. I hired two girls, required that they provide their own transportation, and had them stay for most of the day. They went with us for field trips and to the pool and the beach. I also required them to each plan one craft activity and one song or game for each day. That helped free me up to provide meals and even get a few minutes of rest.

Remember: You can't just leave a child while you take another child to the bathroom!

Field Trips and Activities

Have some car games ready and perhaps bottled water for your time in the car. Having a small snack available is a good idea also. I also recommend having zip-loc bags and paper towels in the car just in case someone is carsick.

Though your specific field trips and activities will be dependent on what is available near you, I have included some of the things we have done to get you started on your planning. Obviously, your outings will depend on your interests and availability, but these ideas may help you get started.

Don't forget to schedule some quiet time after expending lots of energy on a Field Trip.

Watching a movie after a hard day of play

Museums

in Chicago: Museum of Science and Industry, Children's Museum at Navy Pier, Museum of Natural History, Aquarium, Chicago History Museum, Art Institute

in SC: Huntington Beach State Park in Murrells Inlet, SC

You can see lots of alligators and enjoy the Huntington's beach house, Atalaya.

Gardens

e.g. Brookgreen Gardens in Murrells Inlet, SC

This was a good opportunity for the kids to run a little bit. They enjoyed the statues, sculptures, and most of all the butterfly pavilion.

PQ, Sydney, Ellie, Andrew, and Sofie saying the Pledge of Allegiance along with the statue children at Brookgreen Gardens

Available in almost any community:

Fire Station Tour

Fireman from Midway Fire Department talking to campers

Our local fire station has wave runners that were a big attraction for the kids. I set up an appointment. The firemen were wonderful and gave the kids coloring books and some stickers. Be sure to take cookies as a gift.

Bookstore or library

My friend Kirby takes her kids to a bookstore the first day of camp. That way, she makes sure everyone has something to do during quiet time.

Movies

Be sure to find one that is age appropriate for the youngest in your group (you don't want to invite nightmares.)

Bowling

Many bowling alleys offer special rates in their off hours.

Ours has a game arcade attached to it that was a huge hit.

Miniature Golf

Though we have never played miniature golf, we talk about it every year. I think it would be a good outside activity. Remember the insect repellent!

Special Attractions and/or Tours

Again, subject to availability in your area:

Ropes Course - This would be very dependent on the age of your children.

Wonder Works - Interactive exhibits in a building that looks like it is upside down.

Wax Museum - This would be a terrific photo opportunity.

Carriage Rides - Central Park in NYC would be a great place for a carriage ride. Charleston, SC, and New Orleans, LA, would be fun as well. If you live near a farm, you might be able to have an old-fashioned hayride.

Butterfly House - The kids loved the Butterfly Pavilion at Brookgreen Gardens. **Zoo or Aquarium** If your area has a zoo, that is a great outing. Just remember to have plenty of adult help so no one wanders off. Of course, remember sunscreen also.

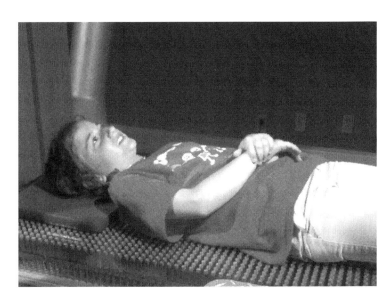

This is Sofie on a bed of nails at Wonder Works.

40

Ghost Tour - Though the children talked about this for days, they were a little freaked out about it. Ellie was the first one to ask to go back to the car with Grandpa; the others bailed when we got to the cemetery just as the sun was setting. It took a lot to assure them that our house is not old enough to have ghosts and we could actually sleep there that night!

*Grandpa with PQ, Ellie, Sofie, Sydney, and Andrew
before The Ghost Tour*

Touristy type shows.

We live near Myrtle Beach and have access to a few different shows. HOWEVER, the drive time is nearly an hour. Once we had more than two children, the noise factor in the car became quite unpleasant. My husband did NOT cope well with that. In following years, I kept our drive time to a minimum when my husband was going with us. Remember car games, water, and snacks.

While You're in the Car

We played "I Spy With My Little Brown/Blue Eyes Something… (Name the color of an item)." Everyone gets a chance to guess and the winner gets to go next. We also played the alphabet game where you have to find letters of the alphabet in order on signs and call them out. We would all get upset when we saw an X at the wrong time!

Another possibility is the "I'm Going on a Trip" game. The first child says I'm going on a trip and on my trip, I'm going to take….(name an item)." The next child says, "I'm going on a trip and on my trip, I'm going to take… name the first item and then add one." Keep going until no one can remember the whole list. One more game is to see how many states' license plates you can see on your outing.

HINT: I would limit field trips to one or two in a 5 day camp. Most of your fun will be close to home, and you will save your energy keeping track of your group in a controlled setting.

Games

In the Pool…….. diving toys, swim rings, noodles

Swimming games that the counselors taught them

NOTE: We didn't have anyone under six years old that year. With two teen-agers and myself in careful attendance, I was comfortable we weren't in any danger. Our available swimming pool does not have lifeguards, but my teen-age helpers were both very good swimmers. You may want to require some sort of swimming test before you allow the kids into the water. This would be true at the beach as well. I found that we played in the sand at the beach and saved our swimming for the pool.

Camp counselor with Sofie and Andrew

At the Beach……. Boogie boards, buckets, shovels

(I recommend at least one real shovel for a big dig!)

Candy Ball Game

This has been a favorite for the last two years. I found the original idea on Pinterest and have modified it slightly.

Preparation: Have dice and a small box or metal lid to roll the dice in. Gather pieces of candy and a few small presents/toys. I used a small bell for the center of the ball the first year and a little Christmas ornament the second year. Wrap the first item in bubble wrap and tape it with packing tape. Then place a piece of candy on the little ball and wrap in bubble wrap and more packing tape.... Use lots of packing tape throughout the process. Continue placing candy or small toy on ball and wrap with more bubble wrap and more tape. Keep the ball shape. Continue to use tape to seal and make the game more difficult. Do not use Saran Wrap or regular tape as the ball will rip too easily.

To Play: The youngest player holds the ball and starts removing the layers. The player on their left is rolling 2 dice as fast as possible trying to roll doubles. As soon as the player rolls doubles, they pass the pan and dice to their left and they get the ball. Player one keeps any treats that came out of the ball during their turn.

I used a metal cookie tin lid to keep the dice contained. The sound of the dice rolling on the metal added to the excitement.

You may need to compensate for younger players. Perhaps the older kids could wear gloves. Or an adult could help the youngest ones. In 2016, I added a grab bag with a few treats inside. If a child did not get anything on their turn, they reached inside the grab bag and got a treat.

Minute It To Win It Games

These are based on the TV show and provide a great way to use bits of time or when you need to refocus everyone. Each participant gets one minute to complete the task. For most of the games such as Shake It, Shake It, Baby, everyone works at the same time. The Peanut Butter/ Ping Pong Balls and Soda Cans on Plate are completed one at a time.

A few examples of Minute It To Win It games:

Peanut Butter Bread/Ping Pong Balls

Spread peanut butter on a piece of bread. I put the bread on a plate. Players stand back from the bread and toss ping pong balls at the bread. The contestant who gets the most balls to stick on the bread is the winner.

Soda Cans On Plate...On Water

Fill a very large bowl with water. Place a plastic plate on the water. Contestants try to stack empty soda cans as high as possible. Have 5 cans available.

Cookie On Forehead

Place a small cookie or cracker on child's forehead. The object is for them to get the cookie into their mouth......NO HANDS ALLOWED.

Pick Up Marshmallows With Chop Sticks

I got chop sticks and take out containers from our local Chinese restaurant. Use one or two small bags of marshmallows. Spread them in middle of table. Contestants place as many marshmallows in the containers as possible in 1 minute. Chop sticks can be held in only one hand, and other hand must remain in the lap.

Shake it, Shake it Baby

We were all laughing too hard to take a single picture. Empty flat tissue boxes and place at least 6 ping pong balls (surprisingly available at most grocery stores) in each box. Remove most of the clear plastic that keeps tissues in place. The object is for the children to shake, shake, shake the ping pong balls out of the box. I used Velcro strips to adhere the boxes to the back of their shorts, but you can use belts. In that case, you would cut a slit in the tissue box and thread the belt through. I didn't have enough small belts for 9 grandchildren so I came up with the Velcro idea.

Pasta Pick Up

Place small pasta rolls (5-6 per child) on table. Child has to pick up pasta using a spaghetti piece in their mouth. No hands allowed.

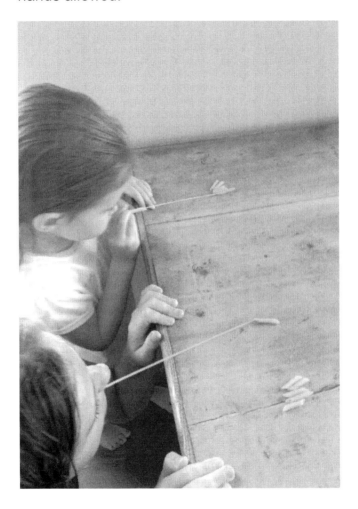

Sofie and Audrey playing Pasta Pick Up

Board games/Card games

Examples: Spot It, Monopoly, Clue, Uno, War, Bingo

Try to pick games that won't overwhelm the youngest or bore the oldest. You could have a game night and divide the children into groups by age. If you have younger children, you can add Chutes and Ladders, and a couple of other well-known children's games.

Puzzles

I set up a table in the living room with puzzles available. Though this has been a big hit in other years, the puzzle table didn't attract much interest in 2016. I have already purchased a few new puzzles for the younger children for 2017.

Scavenger Hunt /Picture Hunt

One year during a family vacation, my husband and I took a walk and figured out some things the kids could search for such as a basketball hoop, purple flowers, a map of our location, etc. The family who returned with pictures of the most items we had specified won. We did not set a time limit. You could also spell out a word like CHICAGO or BEACH or GRANDMA or your family's last name and ask the kids to bring back items that begin with those letters. Obviously, they need adult supervision so it is ideal for a family camp or if you have enough counselors to divide into teams.

Family Vacation Trivia game

One of our grandchildren (Ellie) invented this game on an earlier vacation and introduced it to the whole group in 2014. On the last night, each person writes down 3 questions about things that happened during Cousins Camp (such as, Who won Clue the first time we played?). They can't answer the questions they turn in. We keep score and the person with the most right answers wins the game. Our game leader even had a bookmark she made as a prize.

There was lots of laughter as Grandpa got almost every answer wrong! With such a large group, I think it would be a good idea to limit the number of questions to avoid game fatigue.

Arts/Crafts

I have always used a mixture of purchased kits and from scratch activities.

Camp Counselor with Andrew and Sofie

Painted items

Turtles, banks, boxes, rocks

Remember: These can be sleep dust presents for the night before you plan to use them.

Stepping Stones

You can purchase these at WalMart, local hardware stores, or Amazon, etc.. The kids mix up the ingredients in a big bucket and then decorate them with rocks, buttons, etc. We have placed ours in the back yard. It is fun to add one every year.

Puppets:

One year I purchased cute puppet sets. In 2014, we had wooden spoon puppets (much cheaper!). Of course, you can use old socks, yarn, buttons and make your own puppets. You could put together a short puppet show and perform it for the parents on Skype or in person if you are all together. Keep your story line simple and allow for ad lib.

Sofie with hand made puppet

Perler Beads

These are available at WalMart and other stores as well. I ordered from Amazon. This is a very popular activity, but it does require adult supervision, especially in the ironing of the beads. When each project is done, it needs to be moved very carefully so as not to disturb the tiny little beads before they get ironed and set.

Mosaic Picture Sets

These can be purchased for different age groups so the kids can all work at their level at the same time. I have purchased from WalMart and Oriental Trading Company. For next year, I have a set of butterflies and set of robots.

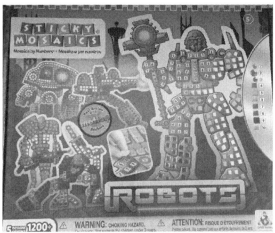

Lava Lamps

I saw this idea on Pinterest (link to directions on this site: http://www.the36thavenue.com/diy-lava-lamps-tutorial/)

You will be able to find easy directions for many projects on the Internet, which is a great source of craft ideas.

PQ with his home made lava lamp

Dream Catchers

Dream catchers are a Native American tradition. The are intended to protect a sleeping person from bad dreams while letting good dreams get through. They are usually made with a hoop that is decorated with leaves, feathers, beads, etc.

I LOVED this project but it was not the kids' favorite. Part of the problem was I didn't have enough help the day we did them, so kids were kind of on their own. Again, I found directions on Pinterest.

Quilted Placemats

I am lucky enough to have a friend who offered to quilt placemats for all 9 children. She provided all the material, the paint (to be sure I had the right kind), and the prepped set-up. The only tricky part for me was to find a good place for the mats to dry. My friend then did the quilting. All the placemats turned out really nicely.

All the placements turned out great.

Other project ideas include quilted purses for the girls and small duffles for the boys (2015) , pillowcases embroidered with their names (2016), and monogrammed beach towels. I bought the beach towels on sale during the winter, of course (2017).

Sand Art Bottles

These are always a big hit. The kids create cool layers of colored sand that can be striped or swirled. The container is filled to the top, and a cork holds the design in place. We have made bottles and necklaces.

Kits can be purchased at arts/crafts stores, Amazon.com, or very cheaply at Oriental Trading Company.

Hint: Try to have a few extra funnels available.

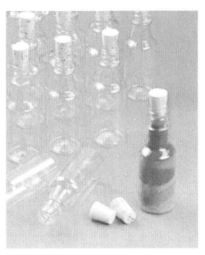

Craft Supplies

Have lots of crayons, markers, paper (all sizes) available.

 HINT: If you don't already stock these things, you can often find them at garage sales or thrift shops if you don't want to buy them new. The kids really like the big rolls of paper so they can outline themselves and each other. Doctors offices use thin paper for their exam tables. You might be able to convince your doctor to sell you one.... Try asking the receptionist. Arts/crafts stores and Amazon also sell paper by the roll.

Water Shooter Art

One of our art projects for 2015 was painting designs on a long roll of paper with water shooters. Instead of water, fill the shooter with paint. The kids loved this. It works best with small water shooters. It is important to use washable kids paint and for the children to wear old clothes. I put garbage bags over their shoes and used a rubber band to keep the bag in place. This is an OUTSIDE activity.

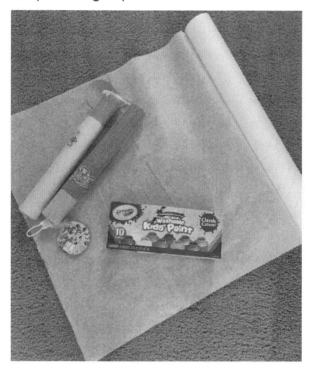

Large roll of white paper with kids paint and water shooters

Name tags

In 2015, I added name tags. The camper's name is on the front with the year and the words Cousins Camp. All the activities are listed on the back. At the end of each day, I mark off the activities each child participated in. If they complete all the activities, they get a small prize at the end of the week. In 2017, I included only two Craft opportunities because some of the older children were outgrowing our crafts. I still had many crafts available, but I added one more Have Fun and one more Pool/Beach.

☐ Western Night   ☐ French Night

☐ Chinese Night   ☐ Mardi Gras

☐ Birthday Party   ☐ Candy Ball

☐ Minute To Win It ☐ Minute To Win It

☐ Minute To Win It ☐ Minute To Win It

☐ Craft   ☐ Craft

☐ Craft   ☐ Pool/Beach

☐ Pool/Beach   ☐ Pool/Beach

☐ Have Fun   ☐ Have Fun

Back side of Name Tags

Things To Remember

Use plenty of sunscreen!

Forms:

Though I never did anything formal, I did ask for handwritten notes giving me permission to travel with the children and to seek medical care if necessary.

- Travel permission
- Medical care: include insurance information and any allergies (Parents names and phone numbers should be included.)
- Medicines for the child and specific instructions for usage

Your shopping list:

* No tears shampoo
* Hair conditioner for kids
* Band-aids
* Alcohol scrub/hand sanitizer

    (Hint: relieves itching from mosquito bites also!)

* Kids toothpaste
* Sunscreen (Yes, I know I have said this but

    YOU HAVE TO HAVE SUNSCREEN).

* Insect repellent

    (I really like the wipes for ease of application.)

* Beach toys

* Pool toys

* Extra swim goggles

 * "Sleep dust" presents

> (See section on Sleep Dust)

* Any supplies you will need for games and crafts

* Zip lock bags

> (for possible emergency in car---we have some grandchildren who have motion sickness)

* Wet Ones/ hand wipes

* Hand sanitizer for your purse/car

* Groceries (If at all possible, get everything you will need ahead of time as it would be much easier than taking children with you.)

* Arrange to borrow things you may need and do not have: blow-up beds, card tables, chairs, crib, high chair, booster seats, car seats.

NOTE: bed rails might also be needed.

Packing list

Send a list to each family in plenty of time so the proper supplies can be gathered. I plan to do laundry each day but want to make sure we have a dry swimming suit when we need it and clean pajamas at bedtime. Since the children are coming to South Carolina in the summer, they may not think to pack a pair of long pants or to bring a sweater.

A few suggestions:

2-3 pairs shorts

2-3 t-shirts

2 pairs socks

More than one swimming suit

Swimming goggles

Tennis shoes, sandals, and flip-flops

A sweater or sweatshirt

At least one pair of long pants/jeans

Two pair pajamas

Night time pull-ups if needed

An old shirt to be worn for painting projects

Sunglasses

Hair necessities: comb, brush, ponytail holders, special shampoos/conditioners if needed (I have these things at home, but if they need a specific brand, I ask they bring that.)

Specific toothpaste brand if child requires it

NOTE: If your kids will travel on an airplane with carry-on suitcases, they will have to follow the rules for liquids.

Any "loveys" needed for sleeping. It would be very sad to be far from home without their special blanket or stuffed animal.

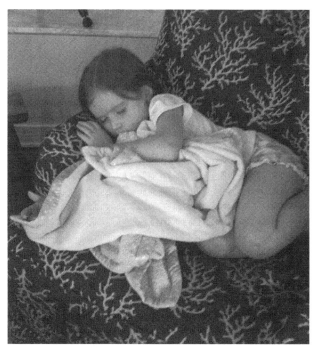

A very tired Audrey after trip to Museum of Science and Industry

Photo Memory Books

Take lots of pictures!

If the children are old enough encourage them to take pictures also. One year, I gave the children disposable cameras so they could take their own pictures.

The first few years, I made multiple copies of each picture I took. Then, I divided them into sets geared for each child. I got little picture albums from my local pharmacy when I saw them on sale for $1.00. Then I compiled each child's book of memories. I hope when they run across them in years to come, they will remember the fun we had. In 2014, I actually forgot to take very many pictures, so we didn't have memory books. It would have been hard to put books together for each of the nine grandchildren. Beginning in 2015, I took lots of pictures and asked the parents to also take pictures and send them to my phone. Then, I compiled the pictures into a book. I used IPHOTO but Shutterfly, Snapfish, or another service such as Walmart would work also. Each family then received one book as a Christmas present.

Food

Note: The Important Thing Is To

Keep It Simple And

Make It Ahead Whenever Possible!

I learned very quickly that it is difficult to really cook 3 meals a day and still enjoy being with grandchildren. Actually, that is true in general! I do my meal planning before anyone arrives and use a yellow pad to keep everything straight. Grocery shopping can take on a life of its own if you haven't planned ahead.

When we have just the grandchildren, breakfast is usually easy: cereal, fruit, toast, juice. In 2014, when we had the whole family, I prepared several breakfast casseroles ahead and saved them in the freezer. Then, I defrosted in the refrigerator for a day, and voila: wonderful breakfast casserole in the morning. Just add fruit, juice, and coffee for the adults.

I plan all the dinners ahead and make out lists so I don't forget anything. I cross check all the recipes and ingredients I will need for those things I am putting together at the last minute. For example, I don't want to start making Ambrosia Salad and not have mandarin oranges.

I don't serve dessert every night. I do keep little boxes of raisins, cereal bars, cheese, crackers, baby carrots, yogurt, and fruit available for between meals. I also make at least one batch of cookies. The White Chocolate Cookies are popular with the members of our family who do not like dark chocolate (See Recipe).

These are a few of the recipes that have worked well in years past:

Spaghetti Pie

Yield: 2 10 inch pies

I make the recipe 1 ½ times for 3) 9-inch pies.

I have had this recipe for MANY years and no longer remember where it originally came from.

Ingredients

- 12 oz spaghetti
- ½ cup butter
- 1 cup freshly grated Parmesan cheese
- 3 eggs, well-beaten
- 2 ½ lbs ground beef (I use very lean---ground sirloin)
- 1 cup finely chopped onion
- 2 cans (15 oz) tomato sauce
- 2 cans (6 oz) tomato paste
- 2 tsp. sugar
- 1/3 cup water
- 1 TBSP oregano
- garlic salt
- basil
- salt
- 2 cups sour cream
- 8 oz shredded mozzarella cheese

Directions

1. Cook spaghetti al dente; drain. Stir in butter, Parmesan cheese, and eggs. Chop well with knife and fork. Form into a crust in 2 buttered 10 inch pie tins. Let cool.

2. Cook ground beef and onion. Drain off fat. Stir in tomato sauce and paste, sugar, water and seasonings. Heat through.

3. Spread sour cream on bottom of spaghetti crusts. Fill pies with meat sauce. Cover with mozzarella.

4. Bake at 350 for 30 minutes.

MAY BE FROZEN

Ellie wearing chef's hat and mustache for Italian night

King Ranch Chicken Casserole

Yield: 8-10 servings

Ingredients

2 pounds skinned, boned, and shredded deli-roasted chicken

2 Tbsp butter

1 medium onion, chopped

1 medium-size red bell pepper, chopped

1 garlic clove, pressed

¾ cup chicken broth

1 (10 ¾ oz) can cream of celery soup

1 (10 ¾ oz cream of chicken soup

2 (10 oz) cans diced tomatoes and green chiles, drained

1 tsp dried oregano

1 tsp ground cumin

1 tsp chili powder

1/8 tsp ground red pepper

3 1/2 cups grated sharp Cheddar cheese

12 (6 inch) fajita size corn tortillas, cut into ½ inch strips

Directions

1. Preheat oven to 350. Melt butter in large skillet over medium-high heat. Add onion, and sauté 6 - 7 minutes or until tender. Add bell pepper and garlic and sauté 3 – 4 minutes. Stir in ¾ cup cooking liquid, cream of celery soup and next 5 ingredients. Cook, stirring occasionally 8 minutes.

2. Skin and bone chicken; shred meat into bite-size pieces. Layer half of chicken in a lightly greased 13 x 9 inch baking dish. Top with ½ of soup mixture and 1 cup Cheddar cheese. Cover with half of corn tortilla strips. Repeat layers once. Top with remaining 1 cup Cheddar Cheese.

3. Bake at 350 for 55 minutes to 1 hour or until bubbly. Let stand 10 minutes before serving.

MAY BE FROZEN

Based on a recipe from Southern Living Magazine

Chicken Quiche

Ingredients:

10" pie crust

1 pkg. chopped spinach—cooked and drained

1 cup cottage cheese

2 eggs, beaten

1 tsp. caraway seed

1 tsp seasoned salt 1/4

tsp. pepper

dash nutmeg

Parmesan cheese..... I use liberal amount

Paprika...use sparingly.

Butter

May add:

2 whole chicken breasts (cooked and cut into cubes)

1 package grated cheddar cheese (or mozzarella)

75

Directions:

1. Preheat oven to 350.

2. Mix all together.

3. Fill pie crust. Pie crust is not necessary-- if you want to skip that step, spray pan with Pam or other cooking spray.

4. Sprinkle heavily with Parmesan cheese and a little paprika. Dot with butter.

5. Bake at 350 for 30 minutes.

To serve, cut in wedges.

I usually triple the recipe as it freezes well.

.... This recipe came from a friend over 40 years ago.

Almond Cherry Granola

Yield: Makes about 4 ½ cups   Double for large group

Ingredients

½ cup peanut butter

½ cup honey   1 cup sliced almonds

¼ cup light brown sugar   2 Tbsp chia seeds

½ tsp ground cinnamon   1 tsp. sea salt

1 tsp vanilla extract   ¾ c. dried cherries

3 cups rolled oats   (can use Craisins or

                                                            other dried fruit)

Directions

1. Preheat oven to 325 degrees. In small saucepan over low heat, mix peanut butter, honey and sugar until mixture is soft and combined, about 3 minutes. Remove from heat and stir in cinnamon and vanilla.

2. In a large bowl, toss together oats, almonds, chia seeds and salt. Add peanut butter mixture over oat mixture and toss well. Make sure oats, almonds and seeds are well coated.

3. Spread mixture onto a rimmed baking sheet in a single layer. Bake, stirring once halfway through until golden brown, about 20 minutes. The mixture will be soft when you remove it from the oven but will become crunchier. Cool on baking sheet, then stir in cherries (or Craisins or other dried fruit).

4. Store in airtight container for 3-4 weeks.

Based on a recipe from The Wall Street Journal

Ambrosia Salad

There are many available recipes for this type of fruit salad. The kids all thought it was DELICIOUS. And, it can be put together quickly. You can use colored mini marshmallows for the wow factor.

BBQ Pulled Chicken Sandwiches

Yield: Serves 6

Ingredients

- 1 small to medium yellow onion, thinly sliced into half moons
- 2 pounds boneless, skinless chicken breasts, fresh or frozen
- 1 cup ketchup
- 2 tablespoons apple cider vinegar
- 1 tablespoon Dijon mustard
- 2 tablespoons molasses (I used brown sugar)

- 1 teaspoon onion powder
- 1 teaspoon cumin
- 1/2 teaspoon garlic powder
- 1/2 teaspoon Tabasco sauce
- 1/2 teaspoon salt
- Whole wheat hamburger buns or rolls

Directions

1. Scatter the onions on the bottom of a slow cooker. Place chicken on top of the onions.

2. In a medium bowl, combine the ketchup, vinegar, mustard, molasses, onion powder, cumin, garlic powder, Tabasco and salt. Pour the sauce over the chicken. Cover the slow cooker and cook on low until the chicken is fork-tender and the sauce has thickened slightly, about 5-6 hours (add an additional hour if using frozen chicken breasts).

3. Remove the chicken from the slow cooker and shred the meat. Return it back to the slow cooker, mixing it with the sauce. Serve the chicken hot on whole wheat rolls, if desired.

Recipe Source: adapted slightly from All You Magazine, August 26, 2011

Reprinted with permission from Mel's Kitchen Café. You can find her food blog at melskitchencafe.com

My crock pot is large, so I tripled the recipe. This was not the only entrée, but we had plenty for dinner one night, snacks, and lunch another day.

French Toast

Use challah (braided braid) or brioche for best French toast. I just slice bread and dip into milk and then a mixture of slightly beaten egg with a little cinnamon. Fry in pan with a little butter; turn over to fry other side. Serve with butter and/or syrup. Heat syrup in a small pot, adding a can of mandarin oranges. You could also use fresh blueberries. Serve over toast.

Blintzes Casserole

Ingredients

- 1 doz. frozen blintzes (assorted)
- 1/4 lb. butter or marg.
- cinnamon
- 6 eggs
- 3/4 c. sugar
- 2 1/4 c. sour cream
- 1 1/2 tsp. vanilla

Directions

1. Defrost blintzes.
2. Melt butter, put in lasagna dish.
3. Arrange blintzes (Alternate types. For example: Place one blueberry, then one strawberry, then one cheese). You can use all of one kind if desired.
4. Sprinkle cinnamon over.
5. Beat eggs.
6. Add sugar slowly.
7. Stir in sour cream and vanilla.
8. Blend well.
9. Pour over blintzes.
10. Bake at 350. Check to see if it is bubbling after 45 minutes but it will probably take 1 hour or a little more.

NOTE: Can be frozen. You can freeze after putting it all together or after baking.

I have had this recipe for 30 years and no longer remember where it came from.

Eggs In A Blanket

I used to make this for my children on the first day of school every year. I thought I made this up, but I saw it named in a blog a few years ago. Just cut out  the center of a piece of bread. Heat a skillet; add a little butter. Place the bread in the skillet and crack the egg into the opening. Cook for a bit (depending how runny you want your egg) and flip over. Cook until bread is lightly browned and egg is done the way you like it.

Monkey Bread

Ingredients

- ½ cup granulated sugar
- 1 teaspoon cinnamon
- 2 cans (16.3 oz each) Pillsbury™ Grands!™
- Homestyle refrigerated buttermilk biscuits
- ½ cup chopped walnuts, if desired
- ½ cup raisins, if desired
- 1 cup firmly packed brown sugar
- ¾ cup butter or margarine, melted

Directions

1. Heat oven to 350°F. Lightly grease 12-cup fluted tube pan with shortening or cooking spray. In large - storage plastic food bag, mix granulated sugar and cinnamon.

2. Separate dough into 16 biscuits; cut each into quarters. Shake in bag to coat. Arrange in pan, adding walnuts and raisins among the biscuit pieces.

3. In small bowl, mix brown sugar and butter; pour over biscuit pieces.

4. Bake 28 to 32 minutes or until golden brown and no longer doughy in center. Cool in pan 10 minutes. Turn upside down onto serving plate; pull apart to serve. Serve warm.

Note: This is the recipe found on the biscuit can.

Almond Pastry

Ingredients:

- 2 packages refrigerated crescent dinner rolls
- 8 ounces cream cheese
- 1 egg, separated
- 2/3 cup sugar, plus more for sprinkling
- 2 teaspoons almond extract (don't use imitation)
- 1 (2 ounce) package sliced almonds
- 2-3 Tbsp. strawberry jam (can use raspberry jam or orange marmalade)

Directions

1. Preheat oven to 350.

2. Unroll 1 package of crescent rolls and place across bottom of a 9x13 pan. (4 rectangles fit across the short way.) Press or stretch lightly to fit, and pinch perforations together to seal.

3. Mix cream cheese, egg yolk, almond extract and sugar.

4. Spread over 1st layer.

5. Unroll 2nd package of crescent rolls and stretch to fit over the top.

6. Slightly beat egg white and brush on top layer of crescent rolls. Brush jam over all.

7. Sprinkle with additional sugar, then sliced almonds.

8. Bake 20-25 minutes, till golden brown.

9. Cool completely before cutting.

Original source of recipe unknown.

Make-Ahead Sausage And Egg Breakfast

Ingredients
- 1 (14-inch) loaf Italian bread, ends trimmed
- 1 1/2 pounds bulk pork sausage
- 1 small onion, chopped fine
- 3 cups shredded extra-sharp cheddar cheese
- 12 large eggs, lightly beaten
- 4 cups 1% milk
- 1 ½ teaspoons table salt
- 1 teaspoon pepper
- 1 tablespoon hot sauce

Directions
1. Adjust oven racks to upper-middle and lower-middle positions and heat the oven to 400 degrees F. Slice bread in half lengthwise then slice each half

into ½ inch-thick slices. Spread the bread in single layers on two rimmed baking sheets and bake until golden, 10-15 minutes, flipping bread and switching and rotating sheets halfway through (or bake one sheet pan at a time). Take care not to let the bread burn - it should be golden brown and toasted. Let the bread cool for 15 minutes.

2. In a large skillet over medium heat, cook the sausage and onion until the pork is no longer pink, breaking the meat into bite-sized pieces as it cooks.

3. Lightly coat a 9X13-inch baking dish with cooking spray. Shingle half of the bread in the prepared pan so that the edges overlap slightly. Top with half of the sausage mixture and 1 cup cheese. Repeat with remaining bread, remaining sausage mixture, and remaining cheese.

4. In large bowl, whisk eggs, milk, salt, pepper, and hot sauce together. Pour evenly over the assembled casserole. Place the casserole on a rimmed baking sheet and wrap the casserole with plastic wrap, pressing the plastic wrap lightly on the top of the casserole. Fill another 9X13-inch dish with cans of food (beans, fruit, whatever) and nest the weighted dish on top of the assembled casserole. You'll be glad you placed the assembled casserole on a

rimmed baking sheet at this point as there may be a bit of spillage over the sides as the casserole compacts. This will help the bread soak up the egg mixture. Refrigerate for at least 1 hour and up to 24 hours.

5. When ready to bake, adjust oven rack to middle position and heat oven to 350 degrees F. Let casserole stand at room temperature while the oven is heating. Remove weights, unwrap casserole, and bake until the edges and center have puffed and the top is golden brown, about 1 hour. Let it cool for 10 minutes before serving.

> **Recipe Source:** *adapted slightly from Cook's Country.*
> *Reprinted with permission from Mel's Kitchen Café.*
> *You can find her food blog at melskitchencafe.com*

Poached Egg And Avocado Toast

(This was for the adults in our crowd in 2014.)

Ingredients

- 8 eggs
- 8 slices whole grain bread
- 2 avocados
- 8 TBSP shaved Parmesan cheese
- salt and pepper
- sprouts for topping

- 2 tomatoes (slice or quarter them)

Directions

1. Use your preferred method to poach eggs. This is my suggestion: Bring large pot of water to boil. Use enough water to cover the eggs when they are on the bottom. (You should do this in batches depending on number you are making).

2. Drop the metal rims (outer rim) of 4 Mason jar lids into the pot. They should lie flat. When water boils, turn off the heat and crack the eggs into each rim. Cover the pot and poach for 5 minutes. If you want softer eggs, poach for 4 to 4 1/2 minutes.

3. While the eggs cook, toast the bread and smash a piece of the avocado on each piece of toast.

4. When eggs are done, use a spatula to lift eggs out of water. Pull the rim of the eggs and place egg on top of toast. Sprinkle with Parmesan cheese, salt, pepper, sprouts.

5. Serve with tomatoes.

Based on a recipe from
Pinch of Yum(pinchofyum.com)

White Chocolate Oatmeal Craisin Cookies

Yield: Makes 3-4 Dozen Cookies

Ingredients

- 1 cup (2 sticks, 16 tablespoons, 8 ounces) butter, softened to room temperature
- 1 1/3 cups light brown sugar (9.25 ounces)
- 1/2 cup granulated sugar (3.5 ounces)
- 2 large eggs
- 2 teaspoons vanilla
- 1 cup coconut (3 ounces)
- 2 cups rolled oats (8 ounces)
- 2 cups flour (10 ounces)
- 1 teaspoon baking powder
- 1 teaspoon baking soda
- 3/4 teaspoon salt
- 2 cups white chocolate chips (12 ounces)
- 1 - 1 1/2 cups Craisins (2-3 ounces)

Directions

1. Preheat the oven to 350 degrees F.
2. In a large bowl with a handheld electric mixer or in the bowl of an electric stand mixer fitted with the

paddle attachment, cream together the butter and sugars until light and fluffy, 1-2 minutes.

3. Add the eggs and vanilla and mix for another 1-2 minutes until the batter is light and creamy.

4. In a separate bowl, whisk together, the coconut, oatmeal, flour, baking powder, baking soda and salt. Add the dry ingredients to the wet batter and mix for a minute or so. With dry streaks remaining, add the white chocolate chips and Craisins and mix until combined.

5. Drop the batter by rounded tablespoons onto a lightly greased or parchment/silpat-lined baking sheet, about 2 inches apart.

6. Bake for 10-12 minutes.

Reprinted with permission from Mel's Kitchen Café. You can find her food blog at melskitchencafe.com

...And Lots Of Fruit & Cereal

Andrew helping out with the orange juice

And yes, we had corn dogs for breakfast one morning. Remember, we are creating memories, not lifetime eating habits.

Theme Nights Menus:

Hawaiian Luau

Barbecued Pork and Barbecued Ribs from local barbecue take-out

Ham Sandwiches on King's Hawaiian Rolls

(made ahead and frozen)

Ambrosia salad,

Cucumber salad

Coconut cake

7-Up tinted blue with Swedish fish candy floating in cup

Italian

Pizza, meatball subs from local pizza place

Salads

Cannoli from local grocery store

Mexican

We looked at the menu online and adults ordered what their family wanted to eat.

French

Chicken Quiche (see recipes)

French bread

Fruit

I have a few sparkly Eiffel Tower centerpieces that are left

from a dinner I hosted for my book
club. I already had paper plates with
drawings of the Eiffel Tower and
some cute pink napkins. I even
found little candy boxes shaped like
the Eiffel Tower and was able to
order some labels that said Cousins
Camp.

Chinese

Order out from our local Chinese restaurant.

I have a few Chinese lanterns, necklaces with Chinese symbols, a game, and shiny red paper tablecloths.

Western

Barbecue Chicken Sandwiches (see Recipes)
Coleslaw and/or green salad

I had red-checked paper tablecloths and I found an old cowboy hat that I had the kids put on when the go to the "outhouse." That was popular and worth a few laughs. The kids waited in line for the "outhouse" experience.

Mardi Gras

Jambalaya

Corn bread (I made jambalaya and the corn bread ahead and froze them.)

Shrimp boil

Salad

King cake (I ordered from kingkingcake.com)

I had lots of bead necklaces, masks, bracelets, noisemakers, green/purple/gold tablecloths, and a party sign to hang on doorway.

Some supplies for 2015

Birthday

I gave each family the book Backwards Birthday Party by Tom Chaplin and John Forster as their sleep dust present the night before our birthday celebration. The book gives many ideas for celebrating in a backwards way: say good night in the morning, eat birthday cake before the meal, say goodbye as you enter a room and hello as you leave. Our grandchildren came up with many ideas of their own. Besides wearing their clothes inside out and backwards, they wore glasses upside down and put underwear outside their shorts.

I made casseroles ahead of time. We had several salads (including Ambrosia Salad because they love it). Dessert was a sheet cake with all our names on it.

Irish Night

We had a baked potato bar with a huge Irish pub salad. For dessert I made an ice cream bombe. I called it Uncle Mulligan's Ice Cream Bombe and put a shamrock on top.

We had "Kiss Me I'm Irish" sashes along with green table cloths and other decorations I purchased at great discounts after St. Patrick's Day.

List for Meals Cousins Camp 2016

This keeps me organized.

Theme Nights and Menus

Notations: *fix in a.m.*

                     **in freezer (get out night before)*

SATURDAY.... No Theme

       **King Ranch Chicken

       **Sour Cream Noodle Bake

       **Spinach Mushroom Lasagna

       *Ambrosia

       Cucumber Salad (Fresh Market)

       Rolls

SUNDAY... Spanish Night

       **Olive Cheese Bread appetizer and *Cream Cheese and Olive Sandwiches

       **Three Sisters Empanadas and Spinach Cheese Empanadas (No Meat)

       *Gazpacho

       **Arroz Con Pollo

       *2 Spanish Salads

MONDAY... Japanese Night

        Order from Sone Hibachi (Litchfield)

        *Edamame Salad

        Empress Caramel Cake

TUESDAY... Chicago Cubs Night

        **Lou Malnati's Pizza

        Hot Dogs/Buns

        Salads from Fresh Market

        Cracker Jacks

        Ice cream with toppings

WEDNESDAY...Birthday Dinner at a Frank's

(Frank's is the local restaurant where we decided to celebrate Grandpa's 70th birthday].

THURSDAY...Irish Night

        **Irish Hand Pies

        *Irish Pub Salad and Purple Cabbage and Pecan Salad

        *Baked Potato Bar (sour cream, grated cheese, bacon, (Irish) butter, green onion, chicken, broccoli [cooked], ranch dressing)

        **Uncle Michael Mulligan's Bombe ...get out when we sit down to eat

FRIDAY...Carnival Night Order from a Tony's

(local pizza and sandwich shop].

Breakfasts

Scones from PI Bakery,

Cream cheese roll ups,

French toast sticks,

Sausage and veggie casserole,

Sticky bun ring,

Cereals,

Eggs

Fruit

Appetizers:

Dips from Get Carried Away,

Cheese/ Crackers,

Pot Stickers,

Shrimp Dip,

Garlic Butter Crescent Rolls

Favorites

Our Favorite Minute To Win It Games

(Directions can be found in Cousins Camp Book or at multiple online locations)

Cookie on Forehead

Pasta Pick Up

Shake It Shake It Baby

Post It Note Stick On (team game)

Bounce 3 Ping Pong Balls into 3 Glasses

Bounce Ping Pong Balls on Bread with Peanut Butter

Unwind Two Rolls of Toilet Paper (or Colored
        Streamers) at Same Time

Absolute Favorite Activity (if I had to name just one)

Candy Ball ..... See page 43

Our Favorite Crafts

(Directions can be found in *Cousins Camp* or at multiple online locations)

Sand Art Bottles (see page 52 or online locations)

Water Shooter Art (see page 53 or online locations)

Perler Beads

Shaving Cream Painting (I use food coloring instead of paint)

Stepping Stones (such fun to add new ones to a pathway each year)

Our Favorite Theme Nights

Hawaiian (the kids loved drinking ocean water…page 82)

Italian night

Irish night (Kiss Me I'm Irish sashes bought after St. Patrick's Day were a big hit)

Cubs Night (of course, you can use your favorite team)

Meal planning is a snap….

Hot dogs, hamburgers, pizza (I ordered pizza from Chicago!), cracker jacks. Throw in some healthy salads!

Suggested Reading:

The following three articles are extremely interesting and show how important it can be for cousins to vacation together.

Asa, Richard. "Why cousins matter: Tapping these familial bonds fosters insight, fellowship," Chicago Tribune. December 13, 2015

Shellenbarger, Sue. "Vacations that Aim to Turn Cousins Into Friends," Wall Street Journal. May 19, 2015.

Waggenheim, Jeff and Katherine Whittemore. "The unique bond of childhood cousins," Globe Correspondents. July 6, 2015.

Resources

Oriental Trading Company:

www.orientaltrading.com

This is where I purchase most of the "stuff" for our theme nights as well as little prizes for our games. Watch for their sales and free shipping.

Custom Ink:

www.customink.com

This is where I purchase t-shirts. They offer a very easy to use design tool for creating custom shirts, and their associates will help you with your order.

Amazon:

www.amazon.com

This is where I purchase some things for our theme nights as well as some of the craft kits.

Don't forget to shop at local craft and/or novelty stores.

And, of course, you can search for anything on the Internet.

Pinterest:

www.pinterest.com

Pinterest is a great place to find ideas for crafts.

They also have "Boards" by topic so you can find a board like "For Kid Crafts" or "For Kids and Teens" to help you with planning your activities

Michaels

www.michaels.com

They offer a whole section for Kid Krafts on their web site as well as many store locations.

JoAnn Fabric and Craft Stores

www.Joann.com

JoAnn's carries a great assortment of crafting supplies in addition to fabric.

Timeline for Cousins Camp

One Year in Advance:

Note: This extended timeline may be necessary for a camp involving multiple families who have to plan their vacation time far in advance. It can be condensed for a camp involving just a few children. It can be condensed further if the distance to Grandma's house is short. In other words: Do not hesitate to plan your camp in a much shorter timeframe.

- Set your date as soon as possible. With adults in the mix, it is harder to find a time that works for everyone.

- Start watching for sales on crafts, sleep dust presents and purchase when you see what you want. Oriental Trading Company often offers free shipping and great sales. Local craft stores will also discount seasonal items that just might work for your camp.

Two-Three Months In Advance:

- Secure counselors.

- Reserve plane tickets.

- Reserve rental car if necessary.

- Buy tickets for special events.

- Order t-shirts.

- Plan theme nights well in advance so as to start gathering materials you might use.

- Put everything for each theme night in a bag.... I used white garbage bags so I could write on them in big letters. This will prevent you from forgetting that you had some Chinese lanterns for Chinese night. They certainly won't fit in on Western Cowboy night.

One Month In Advance:

- Send packing lists to each family.
- Ask each family for their shopping list requests. For example, we need almond milk, skim milk, whole milk.
- Look for recipes that freeze easily.
- Cook and freeze as much as you can.
- Wholesale warehouses (e.g. Costco, Sam's) offer many pre-prepared, frozen casseroles which you might consider for the convenience factor.

One Week in Advance

- Organize all the linens. Check to be sure you have beds/sheets/towels for everyone. I had to buy a few towels, but we have used them every year.
- Borrow anything you will need.
- Separate sleep dust gifts into bags and mark which night they will be used. Remember to give an art project the night before you want to do it! So, if you plan to do sand bottles on Tuesday, give the supplies on Monday night.
- Send reminder e-mail if necessary to each family asking about specific food requests.

Day Before:

- Do as much grocery shopping as possible. You will have to replenish during the week, but try to cut down on the number of visits to the store...... especially if you will have to take the children with you.
- Be sure you have completed meal lists, theme night lists, sleep dust lists.

Cousin Camp Survey

I wanted to make sure I was making the most of our time together so I devised a survey for our final day together:

COUSINS CAMP SURVEY

1. How important is Cousins Camp to you? Circle your answer (1 is lowest; 10 is the highest).

   1   2   3   4   5   6   7   8   9   10

2. How many years have you attended Cousins Camp?

   1   2   3   4   5

3. Name your favorite game: (possibilities include water balloon toss, bingo, minute to win it games, candy ball....if you choose minute to win it games, which one?)

4.   a. Name your favorite place we have been: (possibilities include Museum of Science and Industry, Wonder Works, Alligator Alley, Brookgreen Gardens, Dolly Parton show, movies, beach, pool) WHY?

       b. Name the place you liked the least. WHY?

5. What was the best craft we have done: (possibilities include dream catchers, lava lamps, presents for parents, painting banks, sand art)

6. Did you have a favorite meal? If so, what was it?

7. What do you think is the best part of Cousins Camp?

8. Is there anything you would like to change about Cousins Camp?

9. What advice could you give someone who is going to attend a Cousins Camp?

10. What advice could you give a Grandma who is planning a Cousins Camp?

One Last Note

So, now you are ready to begin your planning. I hope you will enjoy your time together and find it rewarding. I know your grandchildren will thank you.

Hi, Grandma

I made this for you to show how much I enjoyed going to South Carolina. I also enjoy going to cousins camp. I look forward to it all year. Thanks for having cousins camp! Love, Ellie

About the Author

Jana Hletko is a creative educator, parent, and grandparent. She was one of the first 100 teachers in the United States to attain certification from the National Board of Professional Teaching Standards. With that honor came an invitation to the White House and a meeting with President Bill Clinton. In 1999-2000, she was the Georgetown County Teacher of the Year, and she was the South Carolina Journalism Teacher of the Year in 2005.

She and her pediatrician husband, Paul, have three married children and nine grandchildren. While Jana stayed at home with their children when they were young, she and her husband became interested in child car safety and helped get legislation passed in Michigan requiring child car seats. She then worked for a community hospital in an education program to encourage seat belt and car seat use.

Though the Hletkos are fortunate to live by a beach in South Carolina, their children are in professions that have taken them to the big cities of Chicago and Washington, DC. Jana developed Cousins Camp because she wanted to share special 1:1 time with her grandchildren. She has succeeded in creating wonderful memories that she and her grandchildren will always hold dear.

After being prodded by friends to share her creativity and experience, she wrote this book to help others enjoy the fun and excitement of planning, conducting, and enjoying their own Cousins Camp to spend special time with their grandchildren.

Made in the USA
Lexington, KY
23 April 2019